The Official HIBERNIAN FC Annual 2020

Written by David Forsyth
Designed by Chris Dalrymple

A Grange Publication

ISBN: 978-1-913034-21-4

CONTENTS

WELCOME

from Leeann Dempster, Chief Executive.

Welcome to the Hibernian FC Annual 2020.

As ever, the Annual looks back on the season past and ahead to the season to come.

But this year, more than ever, there is a lot to look forward to. After 28 years of careful and positive stewardship under former major shareholder Sir Tom Farmer and former Chairman Rod Petrie, the Club changed hands in July.

The new man at the helm, US businessman and self-confessed lifelong football fan Ron Gordon, decided Hibernian was the Club for him after a three-year search that took in four countries over two continents. By anyone's standards, that's a lot of searching, and it was the Club's values and attitude on and off the pitch that convinced Ron that Hibs was the right place for him.

Ron is determined that the Club will build on the solid foundations left by Sir Tom and Rod, and I am delighted that I will be working with Ron as we seek to make Hibernian a real and lasting force in Scottish football.

The change in ownership brought to an end one of the longest-lasting custodianships in Scottish football. We should be grateful not only for all that Sir Tom and Rod did while they were in charge, but also for their care in ensuring that responsibility for the Club was passed to someone of Ron's calibre.

On the pitch last season was a mixed bag. An exciting run in Europe, a promising start, a poor spell mid-season, and then a fantastic run when new Head Coach Paul Heckingbottom took charge, sending us up from 8th place to an eventual 5th place finish. Our Hibernian Ladies team enjoyed another successful season, winning the Cup double yet again.

We hope for a strong season this year with Paul at the helm for his first full season in charge, with European football increasingly a target we want to set ourselves each year. We may not always make it, but we will always aim for it.

Off the pitch too, we have enjoyed some real successes. Our Hibernian Community Foundation celebrated their tenth anniversary with a Gala Ball, and this season adorn the front of our shirts with pride as we celebrate all of the work they do in our community.

The unique GameChanger public social partnership with NHS Lothian and others also continues to do wonderful work in the community, not least through its weekly lunch club and free fitness classes, and through the fantastic Edinburgh Cheer Christmas Campaign.

As ever, everyone at the Club continues to work hard to make you – the Club's fantastic support – proud of your Club on and off the pitch.

Enjoy the Annual.

SEASON 18-19 REVIEW

THE EUROPEAN CAMPAIGN:

Through our 4th place finish the previous season, Hibernian were back in Europe, competing in the Europa League.

An exciting run was enjoyed, with the Club winning through two ties before being eventually overcome by the Norwegian side Molde, led at that time by now Manchester United manager Ole Gunnar Solskjaer.

The run kicked off before the league season was underway, with a comfortable aggregate victory over Faroe Islands side Runavik. A 6-1 home win was followed up by an away trip that will live long in the memory, not least for the spectacular location of the tiny away stadium or the 6-4 winning scoreline for a 12-5 overall win.

The next round brought a much more difficult prospect, with crack Greek top flight team Asteras Tripolis higher seeded. The writing looked to be on the wall in the home tie, with Hibs two goals down in the first 35 minutes things looked bleak. However, the second-half saw the tie turn on its head with goals from Efe Ambrose and David Gray topped by an injury time winner from Flo Kamberi that saw the team take the narrowest of leads to Greece.

The second tie, played in the summer heat of Greece, saw Hibernian strike first through a wonderful goal by Super John McGinn and, while Asteras did hit back to equalise in the second half, the Greek side were unable to get the victory on home soil they needed, and Hibernian were through to face Molde.

The Norwegian side promised to be tougher still, and so it proved.

A hard-fought home leg at Easter Road saw the Norwegians celebrate at the end of a nil each scoreline, suggesting their confidence at taking the tie back to their picturesque and fairly remote home.

Their confidence was not misplaced. Despite a decent showing, Hibernian were undone by some clinical finishing to lose 3-0 and the European adventure was over, ending our best run for many years.

THE CUPS:

The team didn't enjoy its strongest run in either the William Hill Scottish Cup or in the Betfred Cup.

The Betfred Cup saw the team given a bye to the second round (the last 16) as the club was competing in Europe. Hibs managed to defeat Ross County 3-2 at Easter Road after falling behind to an early goal by the Staggies. Goals from Gray, Mallan and Horgan were enough to see Hibs through to the next round, the quarter finals.

Paired with high-flying Aberdeen in the quarter finals, but again at Easter Road, Hibernian were unlucky to lose out after the full ninety minutes and extra time ended with the tie goalless. A penalty shoot-out of high quality ended at 6-5 in the Dons favour.

The quarter final stages were to see the team exit the Scottish Cup also, this time at the hands of eventual winners and triple winners Celtic.

The run started with a comfortable 4-0 win against Elgin City at Easter Road, with Kamberi and Mallan both scoring and Horgan nabbing a brace. The following round saw another home tie and another home win, this time 3-1 against Raith Rovers, with Horgan, Slivka and McNulty all netting for the Hibees.

The quarter finals saw all-conquering Celtic come to visit. The Glasgow side had not enjoyed much recent success at Easter Road, but on the night were in good form but it still required two superb strikes from Forrest and then Scott Brown in the second half to put the round to bed, and Hibs out of the Cup.

THE LEAGUE:

AUGUST

As ever August saw the league's opening fixtures, with an opening day win over Motherwell secured by 3-0 thanks to goals from Mallan, Shaw and Boyle. That was followed up by a 1-1 draw achieved away from home against bogey team St Johnstone, and then another 1-1 draw, this time at home against an Aberdeen side which had to defend hard to earn their point.

SEPTEMBER

September opened with a defeat away to newly-promoted Livingston, the Lions proving a difficult nut to crack for all-comers at Almondvale. Despite taking the lead through Horgan, the Hibees were unable to hold out and conceded two second-half goals to leave pointless.

A thrilling home encounter with Kilmarnock was next up, with two early strikes from Mallan and Gray apparently having the team on easy street. Killie had other ideas, fighting back to level by half time. A Flo Kamberi penalty well into the second half would eventually settle the outcome in favour of Hibs. That match was followed by a polished 3-0 win away to Dundee, with goals from Kamberi, Boyle and Agyepong, and a strong month ended with another win on the road, this time a 1-0 win at St Mirren courtesy of David Gray.

OCTOBER

A mixed month was to follow. October saw the team get off to a flier, hammering six past Hamilton without reply, through a Mallan brace, goals from Kamberi, Hyndman and Boyle and an own goal. The next game saw Hibs lose 4-2 to a strong Celtic side at Parkhead, Kamberi and Boyle scoring, and then battle to a hard-fought nil-each draw with Hearts at Tynecastle, finishing with ten men after Kamberi was dismissed.

NOVEMBER

November was to prove even more difficult, as the team suffered a mid-season loss of form. Defeat at home to St Johnstone was difficult to bear as the Perth men scored in the final minute, and then an away trip to Aberdeen also ended in a single goal loss before the month ended with a single point gained through a 2-2 draw at home to struggling Dundee, despite the Hibees being two goals up within half an hour.

DECEMBER

The poor form continued into December with a dismal 3-0 loss away at Kilmarnock, followed by a home draw against a St Mirren side battling relegation. The two Hibernian goals came from youngsters Shaw and Porteous. But the tide started to turn a little, as Hibs managed to beat Hamilton in Lanarkshire by a single goal from Shaw, and that was followed by an outstanding home performance against Celtic which saw the Hibees win 2-0 thanks to goals from Slivka and Kamberi. Rangers came calling next, and a hard-earned nil-nil draw was the result, followed by another tie, this time at home against Livingston with a late leveller from Porteous earning Hibs a point. A trip to Ibrox was next, with a late McGregor goal cancelling out an early Rangers goal and earning another draw against a strong Rangers. However the month and year ended on a more sour note, a 0-1 defeat at home to arch-rivals Hearts earning the Jambos a rare win in recent years at Easter Road.

JANUARY

On their January return from a mid-season break in Dubai, the poor run continued, with a 1-0 defeat away to Motherwell. A win in Paisley against St Mirren followed, with goals by Shaw, McGregor and Mallan securing a 3-1 win after Saints had scored first.

FEBRUARY

But at the start of February another defeat followed, this time at home to Aberdeen, with Hibs scoring first and early through Shaw only to see the Dons hit back twice within 15 minutes, a lead they would hold. A 2-0 defeat to Celtic in Glasgow followed, and then goals from Kamberi and McNulty saw the team defeat Hamilton by the same margin at Easter Road, with new Head Coach Paul Heckingbottom in the home dugout. That was to spark an outstanding run of form. A trip to Dundee saw the Hibees slam four past the home side, with McNulty scoring twice and Mallan and Kamberi also scoring in a 4-2 win, and the month ended with a win – at last – against St Johnstone in Perth, with McNulty again scoring twice in a 2-1 win earned despite being down to ten men with Slivka dismissed.

MARCH

March started with another visit from Rangers, and again the two sides could not be separated – the third draw between the two of the season. A goal from Kamberi cancelled out an earlier Rangers strike, ensuring that yet again the points were shared. The unbeaten run under Paul Heckingbottom continued, with McNulty and Gray scoring in a comfortable 2-0 win against the Steelmen of Motherwell, and March ended with a 2-1 away win at Livingston, Hanlon and Mallan scoring for Hibs.

APRIL

The superb run of form had taken Hibernian from 8th place into European contention, and the strong showing continued into April – although points were to prove hard to come by. A goalless draw against high-flying Kilmarnock opened the month, before a fine away win at Tynecastle saw the team avenge their earlier loss to Hearts at Easter Road. Two goals from an outstanding Daryl Horgan ensured Hibernian regained the derby bragging rights. A tough goalless draw against Celtic at Easter Road was followed by another draw, 1-1, against Hearts at Easter Road with an own goal by Jambo skipper Berra.

MAY

The final month of the season, May, opened with the new gaffer's first taste of defeat, a 1-0 away loss to Rangers at Ibrox. Another away defeat by 1-0 followed at Kilmarnock, and the season ended at Easter Road on May 19th with a 1-2 loss to Aberdeen, with a McNulty strike not enough to gain the points.

The season may have petered out, but a ten-match unbeaten run following the appointment of Paul Heckingbottom promised much more was to come.

SEASON QUIZ

1 Which team did Hibernian defeat despite only finishing with ten men?

2 Name the two sides Hibernian defeated in Europe?

3 Who was new gaffer Paul Heckingbottom's first match against?

4 Who scored twice at Tynecastle to earn Hibernian derby bragging rights?

5 Name the former St. Mirren star who scored for Hibs in a win at Paisley?

6 Which Manchester United legend managed his Norwegian team against Hibs in Europe?

7 Two international goalies played for Hibs during the season. Name them?

8 Which countries did they play for?

9 Which team knocked Hibernian out of the League Cup?

10 Who was the Netflix documentary star who joined the coaching staff at Hibernian?

11 From which club did Marc McNulty join on loan?

12 Where did the team take its winter break in January?

13 Against which team did Hibernian score its highest number of goals in the league last season?

14 Who scored for Hibs in the April 2019 draw with Hearts at Easter Road?

15 What was the team's final finishing position in the league?

16 Who did our Assistant Head Coach represent at International level as a player?

17 Which player left the Club early in the season and helped Aston Villa gain promotion to the English Premier League?

18 Who scored the Hibs goals in a 2-0 win over Celtic at Easter Road?

19 How many games were in Paul Heckingbottom's record-breaking undefeated run?

20 Which two Highland sides were defeated in the Cup competitions?

Answers on pages 58.

A NEW ERA BEGINS

A new era began in July when Ronald Gordon became the major shareholder in Hibernian.

Ron is a successful, self-made businessman who has built and sold a network of broadcasting companies. He is also a lifelong football fan, as well as playing the game at college level in the USA.

As a result of the deal Ron Gordon became the Executive Chairman of Hibernian, the mortgage was wiped out and a seven-figure sum was invested.

At the time Ron said: "Hibernian is a Club that must always strive for excellence, on the pitch and off it. The Club must always want to improve, to be better, to do better. The Club must always seek to serve its supporters, its people, and its communities."

Nothing has made him change his mind, as he continues to look at how he can help the management team, led by Leeann Dempster, bring further improvement to the progress at Hibernian.

"I grew up loving football. I played when I was growing up in Peru, and during the time I spent in Australia. Even when I moved to the US aged 15 I tried to play, even although football had not really grown in the States at that time. I love the game.

"I had sold my business in 2017, and I spent around three years searching for the right Club before I found Hibernian. The more I learned about the Club, the more I knew the people there, its history and its values, the more I knew it was the right Club for me. I fell in love with it."

So who is the new man at the helm of our Club? Apart from anything else, he's a multiple Emmy Award winner – the equivalent of Oscars for TV. That's something few clubs can claim!

Ron was born and raised in Peru and is also proud of his Scottish heritage. His grandfather emigrated to Peru in 1908. Ron studied at Markham College, the British school in Lima, and attributes his upbringing in a football-obsessed nation for his love of the game as player and fan. He emigrated to the United States from Peru at the age of 15.

In business he was the founder and majority shareholder of ZGS Communications, Inc., one of the leading independent broadcasting and media companies serving the Spanish-speaking community in the United States.

The company became the largest independent affiliate group of the Telemundo Network. In April 2009, taking a leave from ZGS for three years, Ron was named President of the Telemundo Station Group at NBC Universal, the largest Spanish television station in the country. Over his many years in the media industry,

Ron received numerous accolades including 5 Emmy Awards, 2 Telly Awards, and a White House Media Achievement Award.

He has a strong belief in community and serving the community. Ron is also a founder and director of John Marshall Bank, one of the leading community banks serving the Washington, D.C. metropolitan area, with assets of over $1.4 billion and considered one of the best managed and most innovative small business banks in the region.

Ron added: "I am honoured and excited to have the opportunity to be a part of the wonderful history and legacy of Hibernian FC. I think we can do something really special at this club, on the pitch and in the communities we serve."

Ron took over the reins from Sir Tom Farmer and former Chairman Rod Petrie. The Club had enjoyed the stable and progressive stewardship of the pair for 28 years.

Chief Executive Leeann Dempster, who has overseen the past five years of progress working first with Rod and latterly with Ron, said: "First, we should acknowledge the tremendous foundations left by Sir Tom and Rod. They transformed the Club's infrastructure and saw a number of sporting successes gained during their time at the helm.

"Ron is absolutely the right person to take us forward over the coming years to build on that legacy. He has a genuine love and passion for the game, he is a successful businessman with great experience, drive and energy, and he has a real desire to bring all of his skills to bear to help us build this club.

"I am genuinely excited about the future. Of course there will be bumps along the way, but I firmly believe we can look forward to a really bright future."

Ron is a member of the Gordon clan, whose motto is "Bydand." That is thought to be a contraction of the old Doric term "Bide and Fecht" or "Stay and Fight." A bit like 'persevere'...and we all know what happens when we persevere!

HIBS KIDS

Hibs Kids tickets provide the perfect introduction to the Club for budding young Hibees in a great value bundle, with memberships available to those aged 11 or under for just £20.

The package includes:

- A ticket to four Hibs Kids matches during the 2019/20 season (or matches remaining post Christmas).
- The opportunity to be a mascot at every Hibernian home league match (2 per match, 11 for Hibs Kids matches).
- A Hibs Kids membership card which can be used to gain access on matchdays.
- A birthday card delivered to your registered address.
- Hibernian FC wallchart and stickers.

Child season ticket holders automatically become Hibs Kids members, and will receive the membership card, birthday card, wallchart and stickers, as well as being in the draw for the mascot opportunity.

HOW TO PURCHASE

Hibs Kids memberships can be purchased online or at the Hibernian Ticket Office.

When purchasing a Hibs Kids membership online please note a new profile will be required for the kid. Their account can then be linked to the main adult for future ticket purchases.

www.hibernianfc.co.uk

SIR DAVID GRAY

"Liam Henderson to deliver... David Gray has scored! The Captain! Hibs are standing on the brink of history!"

Now where did we hear that...?

Oh, that's right, May 21, 2016 – THAT day when David Gray rose to nod in THAT goal. The one that ended 114 years of heartache and pain. The day he scored the goal that won, that finally won, the Scottish Cup. The day Sky commentator Ian Crocker's phrase entered Scottish football folklore.

No wonder then that the club's inspirational captain is revered to the point of being conferred his "knighthood" by the fans. He's "Sir" David Gray to every Hibs fan in the land.

But there is more to the reverence in which Sir David is held than that goal alone – wonderful and historic though it was. It is also about a consummate professional at work, a leader, a warrior, a man who always gives his all for the cause. A man who "gets" the Club and what it means to its supporters.

David was the first signing made by Alan Stubbs in 2014. By the summer of that year, he was club captain, a position he's kept ever since. Now 31, he was offered and accepted a new deal that ties him to the Club until 2023, that will see him transition from first team player to a potential coaching role.

Leeann Dempster, Chief Executive, explained that the Club did not want to lose their inspirational captain altogether. "We wanted to offer David some security and a role he can transition to over the coming years. While he is very much a first team player now, we don't want to lose his professionalism and commitment when that changes. We'd rather act now to provide him with a role that can see him transition and stay at the Club. It's an indication of how highly we regard him."

David said: "It was absolutely a no-brainer for me. It's been a fantastic five years since I've been at the club, I've enjoyed every minute of it.

"It's a real good place to be at the minute, an exciting time for Hibs, and there's a lot of good young boys coming through as well, which is important. I think the club's in real good shape at the moment.

"What's driving me at the minute is the hunger to play football and as long as I'm able to do that, and the manager sees me in his plans, I'll do everything I can to be as good as I can every week, for as long as that may be. But as you get towards the end of your career you do wonder what's next. It's great to have this opportunity, this security, and the chance to put something back."

David Gray file:

- David was born in May 1988.
- He spent much of his career south of the border, first with Manchester United, and then also with Preston North End, Stevenage, and Burton Albion.
- He signed for Hibernian in July 2014.
- David has represented Scotland at under-21 level.
- He is 5ft 11ins tall.
- His header which won the Scottish Cup was scored in the second minute of injury time, with 90+2 now a number written into Hibernian folklore.

PLAYER PROFILES

Goalkeepers:

Ofir Marciano

Ofir Marciano joined in the summer of 2017 following a successful loan deal, helping the Club achieve promotion back to the top flight of Scottish football.

He had previously played for Ashdod in his homeland of Israel, as well as Royal Excel Mouscron in Belgium. Ofir is a full Israeli international and is now regarded as one of the top goalkeepers in the Scottish Premiership.

Ofir is an outstanding shot-stopper and has pulled off some memorable saves, including one against Dundee which won an award as "Save of the Season".

Chris Maxwell

Chris Maxwell signed on a season-long loan in July this year, joining Hibernian from Preston North End.

The 28-year-old Welshman was brought in to provide a real challenge for the gloves to Israeli international Ofir Marciano.

When he was signed, Head Coach Paul Heckingbottom praised his experience, and added: "He's a real presence in goal, with good distribution which will help us playing out from the back. We have an excellent goalkeeper in Ofir, but we weren't looking for someone content to be a number two."

Chris made his professional debut aged 18 for his first club, Wrexham, before moving to Fleetwood Town, and then on to Preston. He has also had loan spells at Cambridge and at Charlton Athletic.

Defenders:

David Gray

David Gray is Hibernian Club captain and right back. For more information on David, see the feature on pages 22-23.

Steven Whittaker

Steven Whittaker has enjoyed a stellar career since coming through the ranks of the Club's academy as part of the "golden generation" along with Scott Brown, Kevin Thomson, Derek Riordan and Gary O'Connor and won the League Cup with the club in 2007.

His move to Rangers soon after that saw him appear in a European final, and he has also played for Norwich in England's top league.

Steven returned to Hibs in 2017, and remains an important member of the squad, with his versatility in a number of positions.

Paul Hanlon

Paul Hanlon enjoyed his testimonial year last season, after ten years of loyal and excellent service to the Club he grew up supporting.

The big centre-half is fast closing in on 400 appearances for the Club, and has twice been the Club's Player of the Year. While his many games have brought many outstanding performances, one moment will live long in the memory.

As a Hibs fan as well as a player, THAT goal in the dying minutes of the Scottish Cup tie at Tynecastle which saw the team recover from 2-0 down to take the tie to a replay at Easter Road, which was won en-route to the famous Scottish Cup win in 2016.

Lewis Stevenson

Lewis Stevenson is the only player to have won both the League Cup and Scottish Cup in a Hibernian jersey.

The long-serving left-back, who had his testimonial the year before Paul Hanlon, has been a mainstay of the team for a decade, winning the approval of every manager during his time at the Club.

A man-of-the-match performance in the 2007 League Cup win was an early career highlight, eclipsed only by being an integral part of the team that gained legendary status on May 21, 2016 when they lifted the Scottish Cup.

Tom James

Tom James joined the Club in the summer of 2019, signing on a three year deal from Yeovil Town for an undisclosed fee.

The right-back was brought in to provide cover and competition for inspirational club captain David Gray. He has represented Wales at under-19 level.

The 23-year-old was the subject of a bid of almost £500,000 from West Bromwich Albion last year, but the deal collapsed when personal terms could not be agreed.

Comfortable on the ball, Tom can also provide cover on the other flank.

Adam Jackson

Adam Jackson joined the Club during the summer on a two year deal

The big defender has represented England at under-19 level, and played for Head Coach Paul Heckingbottom at Barnsley in the English Championship.

At 6ft 2in tall he provides a physical presence, and the 25-year-old has significant experience having been on the books of Middlesbrough, Coventry and Barnsley as well as loan spells at Hartlepool and Halifax Town.

Paul Heckingbottom said: "He is strong in the air and understands how we want to defend and how we look to play out from the back. So, he's ideally suited to the way we like to play."

Ryan Porteous

Ryan Porteous is a star in the making. The young centre-half – he is still only 20 years old – was enjoying an outstanding season until a knee injury in January sidelined him for the rest of last season.

A local boy and a childhood Hibs fan, Ryan enjoyed a successful loan spell at Edinburgh City before making his first team breakthrough at Easter Road.

Aggressive, good in possession and fast enough across the ground, Ryan's strong performances saw him attract the attention of a sports agency run by tennis superstar and Hibs fan Andy Murray, who is now mentor to the young player.

Jason Naismith

Jason Naismith was another late signing during the summer, joining Hibernian on a season long loan from Peterborough. The Scot, a defender, has good experience of the Scottish game with Ross County and St Mirren, where he was a regular team-mate of John McGinn.

Midfielders:

Daryl Horgan

Daryl Horgan was signed in the summer of 2018 from Preston North End on a three year deal.

The Irish international, who can play on the wing or in midfield, played for Salthill Devon, Sligo Rovers and Cork City in the Republic of Ireland, before moving to Dundalk, with whom he reached the UEFA Champions League Play-Off Round.

He became a fans favourite quickly on joining Hibs, scoring twice in his first four games. Two goals in a win against Hearts at Tynecastle cemented his status.

Vykintas Slivka

Vykintas Slivka is a Lithuanian international who signed from Italian giants Juventus in 2017.

He scored on his first start for the team, with a stunning strike at Ibrox to seal a 3-2 win for Hibernian.

During his time at the Club so far, the 24-year-old has made a habit of scoring against the Old Firm sides, something which has endeared "Vicky" to the Hibernian support. He made his international debut in 2015 and has amassed more than 30 caps.

Martin Boyle

Martin Boyle joined Hibs in 2014 during a loan spell from Dundee, before signing in the summer of 2015.

The speedy winger quickly became an integral part of the teams that won the William Hill Scottish Cup and promotion from the Championship back to the Ladbrokes Premiership.

The 26-year-old actually made his senior debut for Montrose against Hibs, in a cup tie, in season 2009-10. His continued progress as a player saw him capped by Australia in 2018.

Stevie Mallan

Stevie Mallan was last season's players Player of the Year, in his first season at Easter Road after signing from Barnsley on a four year deal in the summer of 2018.

The midfielder, who played under Paul Heckingbottom at Barnsley, marked his competitive debut against Faroese side Runavik in the Europa League with a double. His goalscoring – particularly from free kicks – was to be a feature of the season.

The 23-year-old has nine caps for Scotland at under-21 level, and will be hoping to follow up last season's fine start at Hibernian with another strong year and a push for full international recognition.

Scott Allan

Scott Allan's return to Hibernian for a third spell was met with joy by supporters who have enjoyed the midfielders swashbuckling style of play during his previous two stints.

The 27-year-old returned to Hibernian after a frustrating spell at Celtic, having joined the Glasgow side from Hibs in 2015.

For more about Scott, see page 50.

Fraser Murray

Academy graduate Fraser Murray is now a first team squad player, and will be hoping to stay as injury free as he can as he looks to push on and claim a regular starting berth.

Fraser made his first team debut in the Irn Bru Cup tie with Turriff United in 2016, scoring the first goal. Subsequent appearances saw him continue his good run, but injuries have hindered his progress during the past 18 months.

His undoubted talent marked him out as another of our young players, the other being Ryan Porteous, to join Andy Murray's sports agency.

Josh Vela

Josh Vela signed for the Club during the summer.

The composed midfielder was 25 when he signed for the Hibees, and had come through the academy set-up at Bolton from the age of 9. He turned out for the Lancashire team more than 180 times in the Championship and League 1, and also spent some time at Notts County on loan.

Signing him on a three year deal, gaffer Paul Heckingbottom said: "Josh will add energy and a competitive edge to our midfield.

"He is an all-round midfielder with the athleticism to support attacks and play on the front foot, helping us win the ball back.

"He was worth the wait and I'm glad we were patient in order to land him."

Joe Newell

Joe Newell signed a two year deal with Hibernian in the summer, joining after spending four years at English side Rotherham.

The winger and midfielder has extensive experience in the EFL Championship, with both Rotherham and Peterborough, amassing more than 140 games.

Paul Heckingbottom said: "He's come in having played a lot of games at a good level in the English Championship and is a threat either out wide or inside.

"Joe can carry the ball up the park and I think he'll link up well with our other attacking players."

Darren McGregor

Centre-half Darren McGregor is one of the Scottish Cup winning legends still at the Club. For more information on this local boy living the dream, see pages 48-49.

Glenn Middleton

Glenn Middleton – who turns 20 on New Year's Day – joined the Club on loan during the summer.

The flying winger joined from top-flight rivals Rangers. Although born in Glasgow, Glenn has spent most of his career to date down south, and in particular with Norwich City where he went through that club's well-regarded Academy system.

He made 27 appearances for the Glasgow club last season, scoring five goals in the process. He joined Hibernian following the injury to Martin Boyle early in the season. As an ambitious player, Glenn was keen to gain more experience through playing more games in the top flight.

He has represented Scotland at a variety of levels, from under 16 to under 21.

Melker Hallberg

Swedish star Melker Hallberg joined Hibernian during the summer.

The four-times B capped midfielder started his career in his home-town club of Kalmar, and became the youngest-ever Allsvenskan debutant for the club when he made his league bow at the tender age of just 16.

He has subsequently played in Norway, Denmark and with Udinese in Italy before coming to Scotland in the summer. He has played at all youth levels for Sweden and also at B international level.

Comfortable on the ball, strong and with pace and energy, he is an all-round midfielder.

"From what I have seen, I think I will be well suited to Scottish football and I like the passion of the supporters," he said on joining.

Attackers:

Christian Doidge

Christian Doidge joined in the summer, after being admired both by gaffer Paul Heckingbottom and the Club's recruitment team for some years.

The 6' 1" Welshman started his senior career at Southampton, coming through that club's fabled academy system, and has played at a variety of clubs in England and Wales. He joined Hibs from Forest Green, where he had been under contract since 2016. During this time, he also enjoyed a loan spell at Bolton.

He scored almost 60 goals in 107 appearances for Forest Green. Hibernian beat a number of other clubs to his signature, something Paul Heckingbottom described as "a statement of intent."

The gaffer said the player "is intelligent, has good movement, scores different types of goals, can handle himself physically and will press well from the front."

Flo Kamberi

Flo Kamberi, Hibernian's Swiss striker, came to the club in the summer of 2018 following a hugely successful loan spell in the second half of the previous season.

The big striker, capped at under-21 level by Switzerland, joined from Swiss Super League club Grasshoppers. Quick, powerful, and hard-working he is a handful for any defence on his day, and has scored some outstanding goals.

Flo has also played in Germany.

Oli Shaw

This looks likely to be a big year for young striker Oli Shaw.

The academy graduate has already racked up more than 60 appearances for the first team since making his debut under Alan Stubbs in 2015. An excellent finisher, he will be looking to force his way into more regular starts this season.

Oli spent the 2017/18 season on a development loan to Stenhousemuir. This year may well be his breakthrough season.

HIBERNIAN LADIES

Since the last Hibernian Annual went to press Hibernian's women's team has enjoyed another barnstorming, trophy-laden time.

They followed up the previous year's knockout double with another double-cup success in the 2018 season as they stormed to winning the SWPL Cup with a 9-0 win over Celtic and an 8-0 win against Motherwell secured the SSE Scottish Women's Cup in November that year.

In the close season between the two campaigns a number of players left to play professionally in England, including the likes of top scorer Abi Harrison and Scotland international Kirsty Smith, but Head Coach Grant Scott kept a lot of good young players and recruited well.

Perhaps most importantly, at the time of going to press the team which contains many key players such as Jamie-Lee Napier, Shannon McGregor, Joelle Murray, Kirsten Reilly, Siobhan Hunter and Jenna Fife, were able to retain the SWPL Cup with a tense shoot-out victory over Glasgow City at the Penny Cars Stadium in Airdrie.

They have also competed in the UEFA Women's Champions League and qualified for the Round of 32 for the first time since 2016. They topped their group in Slovenia with three straight victories to reach the knockout stages of the competition, which bodes well for the future of the team.

In addition, the summer of 2019 saw two of the club's star players – Jenna Fife and Joelle Murray – named as part of the first ever Scotland squad to make the FIFA Women's World Cup in France.

Goalie Jenna Fife and midfielder Joelle Murray were delighted to be called up to the squad, which was a dream come true for Joelle, who has been with Hibernian since she was just 12 years old.

Joelle skippered the team to its fourth straight Scottish Women's Premier League Cup in May 2019 and then – just a few days later – she took the call she had longed for.

"I just waited patiently for my phone to ring. The call eventually came and after a tense 4 or 5 minutes, Shelley (the Scotland manager) said the words I longed to hear "you're going to the World Cup". I was absolutely delighted and very proud.

"Scottish women's football has come full circle and I've been fortunate to play alongside so many great players – past and present. These individuals, along with so many more, have all contributed to the growth of the game and have created a legacy that will never be forgotten. The women's game in Scotland is growing and I can only see it getting bigger and bigger".

The first half of the season saw them suffer two defeats, but they have kept themselves at the upper end of the table and registered many fine victories – including two 6-0 wins, a 7-1 and an 8-0 savaging of Forfar Farmington.

HIBEE HISTORY

They are supporters, they're volunteers, and they are the guardians of our history and our heritage – Hibernian Historical Trust.

Established in 2004 by a group of fans, the Trust has been created independently from the Club – but with its full backing – as a charity designed to proactively protect, celebrate and share the rich heritage of our club.

Led by its trustees, the group does this by collecting and displaying around the stadium artefacts and memorabilia important to the club's history and to its supporters. It also uses the material to stimulate interest and promote education and entertainment for the public, and their work helps reflect the part played by the Club in the history of Scottish football.

But their work doesn't stop there. The Club's history reflects the social history of Leith, Edinburgh and Scotland – and the uses of the material are rich and varied.

Football Memories is a product of Alzheimer Scotland's pioneering work on their Football Reminiscence project, using memories of football to improve the life of people with dementia. Over 88,000 people in Scotland have a diagnosis of dementia, which is the equivalent of every spectator on an average football weekend.

For the past few years the Hibernian Historical Trust have been holding meetings at Easter Road Stadium, where people with dementia and other memory challenges gather to enjoy talking football and looking back more generally with the help of old photos and other memorabilia.

Club historian Tom Wright starting a tour of the stadium.

The group is open to fans of all clubs, as well as Hibs fans, and they are always well attended and many of the participants have since become lifelong friends.

The Trust is also responsible for the increasingly popular history tour of Easter Road Stadium, with Club Historian and Trust Curator, Tom Wright.

Walk through the dressing rooms, the tunnel, see rare Hibernian shirts and artefacts on display in the Board Room and take in each stand at our home. A perfect afternoon at Easter Road Stadium for any Hibernian supporter.

Tours are priced at £10 per adult, £7.50 per concession and £5 per child, with discounts for large bookings. Group bookings are also available on different dates and times to suit you.

Gift vouchers for the Stadium Tour are available, a perfect birthday or Christmas present for the Hibernian supporter in your life.

For more information on booking tours or purchasing gift vouchers, contact Hibernian Football Club either by phone, 0131 661 2159, or by visiting hibshistoricaltrust.org.uk.

The unique set of Scottish football medals belonging to the great Gordon Smith, still the only player to have won the league with three different clubs, including his wins as part of the Famous Five.

CHRISTIAN DOIDGE

PLAYER QUIZ

1. Who is the Club Captain?
2. Which player signed from Forest Green Rovers'?
3. Name the two players who are mentored by tennis superstar Andy Murray?
4. Which international team does Daryl Horgan represent?
5. Which player is nicknamed Rocky?
6. How many times has Scott Allan signed for Hibernian?
7. Name the Club from which Flo Kamberi signed?
8. Name the two members of the squad who have enjoyed testimonial years with Hibs?
9. Which Hibernian cup winning legend left at the end of the season to join Livingston?
10. Which country did Martin Boyle represent at international level?

Answers on pages 58.

SPOT THE BALL

Can you spot the real ball Christian Doidge just kicked?

Answer on pages 58.

SCOTT ALLAN

INSIDE THE DRESSING ROOM

This year we're giving our Annual readers a glimpse inside the inner sanctum, the first team dressing room at Hibernian Training Centre.

This is where our stars get ready for work day after day, where friendships and partnerships are forged.

But not only that, we're also giving one lucky reader the chance to **win a free personal tour of the training centre for them and their family!**

All you have to do is play the role of team captain, and decide which player should sit where in the changing room. Just fill out the blanked-out place plan, telling us why you've made the choices you have, and we'll get club captain David Gray to judge which plan he reckons is best.

And remember, in the Annual you'll find the very words our stars wanted up on the gym wall to inspire them as they work. They may help you as you decide who sits beside who, and why.

Send your entries:
By email:
frontdesk@grangecommunications.co.uk with HIBERNIAN FC COMPETITION 2020 in the subject line.

By post:
Hibernian FC Competition 2020, Grange Communications Ltd, 22 Great King Street, Edinburgh, EH3 6QH.

Please note: Entrants must provide their full name, age, address and a daytime telephone number in order to make a valid entry.

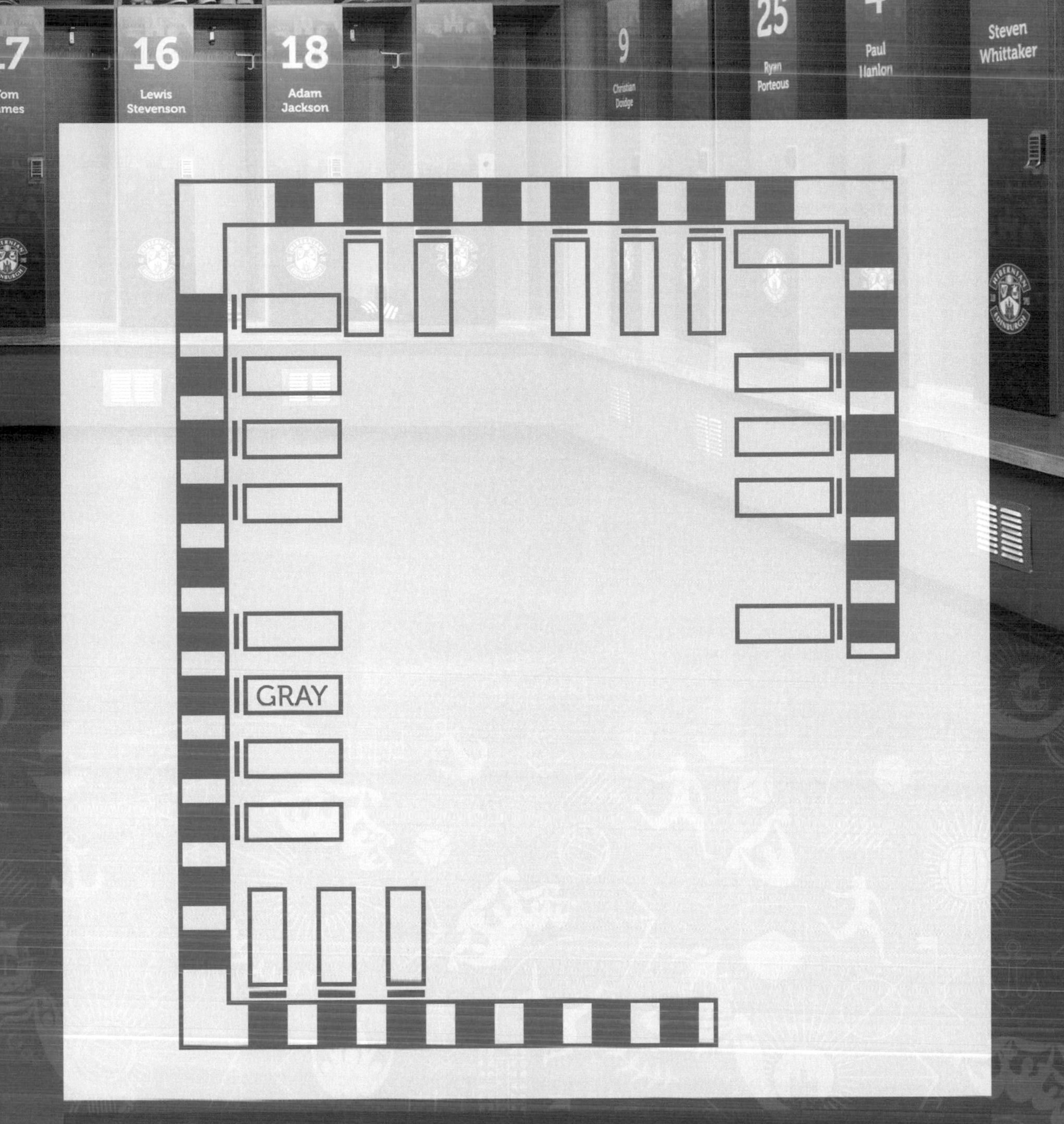

Competition Terms and Conditions

1) The closing date for this competition is Tuesday 31st March 2020 at midnight. Entries received after that time will not be counted.

2) Information on how to enter and on the prize form part of these conditions.

3) Entry is open to those residing in the UK only. If entrants are under 18, consent from a parent or guardian must be obtained and the parent or guardian must agree to these terms and conditions. If entrants are under 13, this consent must be given in writing from the parent or guardian with their full contact details.

4) This competition is not open to employees or their relatives of Hibernian Football Club. Any such entries will be invalid.

5) The start date for entries is 31st October 2019 at 4pm.

6) Entries must be strictly in accordance with these terms and conditions. Any entry not in strict accordance with these terms and conditions will be deemed to be invalid and no prize will be awarded in respect of such entry. By entering, all entrants will be deemed to accept these rules.

7) One (1) lucky winner will win a personal tour of the training centre for them and their family.

8) The prize is non-transferable and no cash alternative will be offered. Only one entry per contestant.

9) The winner will be contacted within 72 hours of the closing date. Details of the winner can be requested after this time from the address below.

10) Entries must not be sent in through agents or third parties. No responsibility can be accepted for lost, delayed, incomplete, or for electronic entries or winning notifications that are not received or delivered. Any such entries will be deemed void.

11) The winner will have 72 hours to claim their prize once initial contact has been made by the Promoter. Failure to respond may result in forfeiture of the prize.

12) We will not share your information with any other companies or use your data other than as necessary to administrate the competition. Once the competition is over your information will be securely destroyed. Your information will always be safeguarded under the terms and conditions of the Data Protection Act 1998.

13) The Promoter reserves the right to withdraw or amend the promotion as necessary due to circumstances outside its reasonable control. The Promoter's decision on all matters is final and no correspondence will be entered into.

14) The Promoter (or any third party nominated by the Promoter) may contact the winner for promotional purposes without notice and without any fee being paid.

15) Hibernian Football Club's decision is final; no correspondence will be entered in to. Except in respect of death or personal injury resulting from any negligence of the Club, neither Hibernian Football Club nor any of its officers, employees or agents shall be responsible for (whether in tort, contract or otherwise):

(i) any loss, damage or injury to you and/or any guest or to any property belonging to you or any guest in connection with this competition and/or the prize, resulting from any cause whatsoever;

(ii) for any loss of profit, loss of use, loss of opportunity or any indirect, economic or consequential losses whatsoever.

16) This competition shall be governed by Scottish law.

17) Promoter: Grange Communications Ltd, 22 Great King Street, Edinburgh EH3 6QH.

NICKNAMES

Match the name to the player:

1. "Rocky"
2. "Kevin"
3. "Sackie"
4. "Hammer"
5. "Vicky"
6. "Jacko"
7. "Daz"
8. "Porto"

Darren McGregor

Ofir Marciano

Vykintas Slivka

Maciej Dabrowski

Adam Jackson

Jamie Gullan

Sean Mackie

Ryan Porteous

Answers on pages 58.

PLAYER CHAT

Which player do his team-mates think...

...Is worst dressed?
Vykintas Slivka (although he thinks it's Stevie Mallan).

...Is the biggest pest?
That would be Boyler again, as nominated by captain Sir David Gray and Darren McGregor.

...Is most likely to spend a long time in front of the mirror?
Flo Kamberi.

...Will eat a Toblerone every time he scores?
Flo Kamberi.

...Is best in the gym?
Daryl Horgan.

...Is learning guitar?
Vykintas Slivka.

...Is the worst singer?
Flo Kamberi followed by Darren McGregor (as nominated by Darren McGregor).

...Rates the five days following the 2016 Scottish Cup Final the highlight of his time at Hibs?
Martin Boyle.

...Is worst in the gym?
Martin Boyle (He's a toothpick according to Stevie Mallan).

...Has scored against England goalie Jordan Pickford?
Flo Kamberi, for Switzerland under-21s.

LOCAL HERO
DARREN McGREGOR

He's the Leith lad living the dream, the boyhood fan now turning out for the team he grew up supporting – Cup-winning legend Darren McGregor.

But it could all have been so different for Big Daz, in lots of different ways.

The stalwart centre-half only came to full-time senior professional football late, well into his twenties, before that playing part-time in lower league and junior football with Cowdenbeath and Arniston Rangers, as well as working in a clothes shop.

And he has also revealed that he almost signed for (whisper it) Hearts at one point! He was approached whilst at St. Mirren, but when Rangers also came in for him he decided to head to Glasgow.

He had spent four years in Paisley and that was followed by a year at Ibrox before, in 2015, he signed for his team, Hibernian.

In the summer, and now 34, he signed a new deal that keeps him at the Club till 2023, as a player and – like his great mate David Gray – transitioning into coaching.

It's a move that delighted Darren.

"It's a stretch imagining playing at 37 just now. I can understand why naysayers would say '37?'

"But I can only tell you how I feel and the way I am as a person, the way I approach every single day with my rehab and my prehab, my diet and just how I look after myself, on and off the field. All these things are factors that are ingrained in me from a young age. I've not just flicked a switch six months ago and said 'I'm going to be this person. I've been this way since I arrived here so I'm hoping the club have seen the good in me and that I have a lot to offer."

As well as mentoring younger players, his new deal requires Darren to promote the Club as positively as he can – something he has done for some time as the GameChanger partnership Ambassador, helping highlight the Club's work in the community he grew up in and loves.

"The Club does great work in the community, and when I can I like to help them highlight that. It's a chance to give something back."

Darren McGregor file:

- He was born in Leith in August 1985.
- He stands over 6ft tall.
- His first senior club was Cowdenbeath.
- He made his SPL debut on 14 August 2010 with St. Mirren.
- He was taken to Paisley by former Hibee Danny Lennon.
- In his one year at Rangers, he was named their Player of the Year.

10 FACTS ABOUT SCOTT ALLAN

Scott is 28 years old, and was born in Glasgow.

His first senior club was Dundee United.

He has 10 caps at under 21 level for Scotland.

Scott has type-1 diabetes and requires daily insulin injections.

This season is Scott's third spell at Hibernian.

He was at the club in the Championship from 2014-2015, winning the PFA Player of the Year award for the Championship.

He enjoyed a six month loan spell at Easter Road in 2018.

He has been signed by 11 clubs in total, 8 of those on loan.

He made his SPL debut at Tynecastle Stadium in an away victory for Dundee United on 31 July 2011, playing 83 minutes.

He was signed by EPL club West Brom in 2012.

SPOT THE DIFFERENCE

There are 10 differences between these two photographs, can you spot them all?

Answers on pages 59.

FITBA' CRAZY!

In the words of the song "We're fitba' crazy, we're fitba' daft..."

The obsessive Scottish passion for football is renowned around the world. While that may not be unique, it can certainly take on a character of its own. Consider the following tales, and let's start with a couple from Hibernian:

Famous Five Great Eddie Turnbull followed his stellar playing career at Easter Road by creating and managing a team many regard as the second best Hibs ever, behind only the Five, the Turnbull's Tornadoes.

Alan Gordon, a notably intelligent player who was a university graduate and a qualified accountant, was told by Eddie Turnbull that "the trouble with you is that all your brains are in your head". Far from being a malapropism, Turnbull was deliberately having fun with the old football adage about "brains in feet." He later claimed that only Gordon and he got the joke.

The great George Best signed for Hibs on a lucrative pay-as-you-play deal in November 1979, earning £2,000 for every appearance in a Hibs shirt, after joining from Fulham for £57,500. During a pre-Christmas clash with Rangers at Easter Road and faced with continual abuse from the visiting supporters, who at one point threw a handful of beer cans at him as he took a corner, the notoriously hard-living Best picked up one of the cans and seemed to take a drink from it.

Laughter could be heard at both ends of the stadium, and Hibs went on to record a 2-1 win.

Brazilian superstar Neymar fell out with the Tartan Army in 2011 following a match between Scotland and the samba stars at Arsenal's Emirates Stadium. A banana was thrown on the pitch, and Neymar – who had been booed by the Scottish fans – claimed the abuse was racially motivated. Arsenal later revealed a teenage German tourist admitted he was responsible for the chucked banana, and also confirmed the piece of fruit actually came from the section reserved for the Brazilian FA's official ticket allocation.

Needless to say the Tartan Army was not amused, but a spokesman suggested to the media he apologise by sourcing a couple of Brazilian starlets with Scots grannies to make up instead.

Hibs fans – along with those of many clubs outwith the Old Firm - have long claimed that Celtic and Rangers get more than their share of the big decisions. During their recent and difficult spell in Scotland's lower leagues Rangers were toiling to a home draw against Alloa when the hilarious shout of "same old Alloa, always cheating" went up. Irony or not? You decide...

Crazy isn't confined to Scotland. In 1998, the Chile defender Javier Margas played three games in England before going AWOL from West Ham for a year, returning the following season with his hair dyed claret and blue to show his commitment to the Hammers' cause.

Or how about this for a short managerial reign. Leroy Rosenior's managerial reign lasted all of 10 minutes in May 2007. According to the media, the press were informed he was appointed as manager. However he claimed he was told 10 minutes later that his services had been disposed of by Torquay United, as the club had been taken over.

And finally, Romanian lower league outfit Steaua Nicolae Balcescu had been threatened with expulsion from the league after a series of pitch invasions and clashes.

Steaua's chairman, Alexandra Cringus, decided the best way to stop the hooligans was by building a crocodile-infested moat around the pitch.

Unsurprisingly local authorities rejected the scheme.

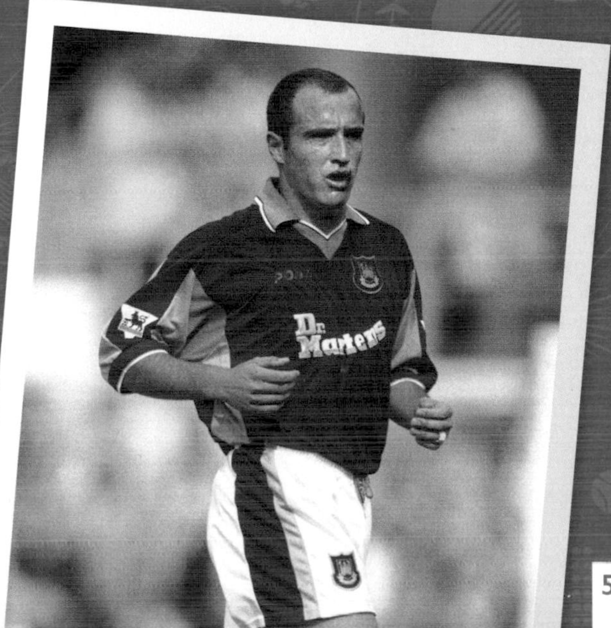

HIBERNIAN WORDSEARCH

Can you find the surnames of 12 renowned Hibernian strikers hidden in the grid below?

R	D	G	F	W	R	Q	N	B	Q	M	L	J
O	Z	M	N	Y	M	O	X	P	F	Z	L	T
N	P	T	N	N	D	N	R	Z	G	D	C	H
N	K	L	G	R	O	E	R	E	K	A	B	M
O	D	N	O	R	S	S	N	N	H	T	Y	R
C	H	G	T	T	I	L	K	T	G	F	L	I
O	K	C	O	R	Z	F	H	C	L	N	L	O
D	U	N	C	A	N	G	F	E	A	M	I	R
T	F	W	L	Y	I	V	T	I	R	J	E	D
Z	Z	K	F	R	N	C	C	K	T	B	R	A
T	H	T	W	C	H	N	H	H	P	H	K	N
P	A	A	T	E	L	A	I	N	E	N	S	M
V	T	X	R	M	K	V	G	Y	N	D	Z	B

Baker
Duncan
Fletcher
Gordon
Griffiths
Jackson
OConnor
Paatelainen
Preston
Reilly
Riordan
Wright

Solution on page 59

PAUL HANLON

CLUB RECORDS AND HONOURS

This year we look at those players who have been record-breakers when it comes to appearing for the mighty green-and-whites (with acknowledgements to Hibernian Historical Trust).

Most overall: **636 Gordon Smith.**
Most League: **449 Arthur Duncan.**
Most Scottish Cup: **51 Arthur Duncan.**
Most Scottish League Cup: **103 Pat Stanton.**
Most Fairs Cup: **23 Eric Stevenson.**
Most UEFA Cup: **15 Arthur Duncan.**
Most UEFA Europa League: **10 Paul Hanlon; 10 Lewis Stevenson**

Youngest: **Jamie McCluskey**
16 years 79 days
(vs Kilmarnock (a), 24th January 2004 - Scottish Premier League)
(Came on as a substitute).

Oldest: **John Burridge**
41 years 163 days
(vs Partick Thistle (h), 15th May 1993 - Scottish Premier Division) (Started match).

Club Honours

Leagues

Scottish Division 1 was the top flight from 1890 – 1975. During that period 4 league titles were achieved, largely due to the renowned team of the Famous Five, during the club's golden period in 1948, 1951 and 1952. An earlier title had been won in 1903. Hibernian have been runners-up on six occasions, in 1897, 1947, 1950, 1953, 1974 and 1975.

The Scottish Cup

The Club has won the Cup on three occasions, in 1887, 1902 and then, of course, on May 21st, 2016, when Rangers were defeated 3-2 at Hampden to end the oldest hoodoo in Scottish football. Runners-up medals have been collected 11 times, illustrating the heartache that was ended in 2016, through teams reaching the final in 1896, 1914, 1923, 1924, 1947, 1958, 1972, 1979, 2001, 2012, and 2013.

Scottish League Cup

Three times Hibernian captains have held this trophy aloft, Pat Stanton in 1972, Murdo McLeod in 1991 and Rob Jones in 2007, with the club runners-up in 1950, 1969, 1974, 1985, 1993, 2004, 2016.

Minor Honours:

The Club has also won the second flight of Scottish league football, now known as the Championship and previously as Division Two, on six occasions – 1894, 1895, 1933, 1981, 1999 and 2017.

The Drybrough Cup was won in 1972 and 1973, the **Summer Cup** in 1941 and 1964, and the **Southern League Cup** in 1944.

QUIZ ANSWERS

P16 Season Quiz:

1. St Johnstone.
2. Runavik and Asteras Tripolis.
3. Hamilton.
4. Horgan.
5. Mallan.
6. Ole Gunnar Solskjaer.
7. Ofir Marciano and Adam Bogdan.
8. Israel and Hungary.
9. Aberdeen.
10. Assistant Head Coach Robbie Stockdale.
11. Reading.
12. Dubai.
13. Hamilton.
14. Christophe Berra og.
15. 5th.
16. Scotland.
17. John McGinn.
18. Kamberi and Slivka.
19. Ten (the best unbeaten start made by a Hibernian Manager in modern times).
20. Ross County and Elgin City.

P41 Player Quiz:

1. David Gray.
2. Christian Doidge.
3. Ryan Porteous and Fraser Murray.
4. Republic of Ireland.
5. Ofir Marciano.
6. Three.
7. Grasshoppers.
8. Hanlon and Stevenson.
9. Marvin Bartley.
10. Australia.

P42 Spot the Ball:

P46 Nicknames:

1. Ofir Marciano
2. Maciej Dabrowski
3. Sean Mackie
4. Jamie Gullan
5. Vykintas Slivka
6. Adam Jackson
7. Darren McGregor
8. Ryan Porteous

P51 Spot the Difference:

Page 54 Wordsearch:

R	D	G	F	W	R	Q	N	B	Q	M	L	J
O	Z	M	N	Y	M	O	X	P	F	Z	L	T
N	P	T	N	N	D	N	R	Z	G	D	C	H
N	K	L	G	R	O	E	R	E	K	A	B	M
O	D	N	O	R	S	S	N	N	H	T	Y	R
C	H	G	T	T	I	L	K	T	G	F	L	I
O	K	C	O	R	Z	F	H	C	L	N	L	O
D	U	N	C	A	N	G	F	E	A	M	I	R
T	F	W	L	Y	I	V	T	I	R	J	E	D
Z	Z	K	F	R	N	C	C	K	T	B	R	A
T	H	T	W	C	H	N	H	H	P	H	K	N
P	A	A	T	E	L	A	I	N	E	N	S	M
V	T	X	R	M	K	V	G	Y	N	D	Z	B

A number of words adorn the wall in the players' gym at Hibernian Training Centre, and they're up there for the players to see day in and day out when they work out.

The words are there to inspire the players – because they are the words the players themselves believe are vital to successful Hibernian teams.

The management team and the players got together to decide on the core values that playing for Hibs should mean. Trust, Confidence, Creativity, Organisation, Teamwork and Winners were the result, and alongside each word are three short sentences that demonstrate what lies behind their thinking.

For example, confidence means not being scared to make a mistake. Organisation means each player understanding his role.

But while the messages are important for the players, they are just as important to young fans.

And if you put all the words together and live by them enough... well that adds up to the image on the other wall and the magic number of 90+2!

90+2
TRUST
Trust in the game plan
Rely on your team mates
Trust everyone is doing their jobs
CONFIDENCE
Want the ball
Believe in yourself and the team
Don't be afraid to make a mistake
CREATIVITY
Express yourself
Make things happen
Try something different
ORGANISATION
Communicate
Understand your roles
Prepare in the right way
TEAMWORK
Make sacrifices
Help each other
Togetherness
WINNERS

WHERE'S
SUNSHINE?